Liquid Cooling Mastery
High-Performance Systems

Table of Contents

Chapter 1. Introduction

In a world increasingly driven by high-performance computing systems, mastering the art and science of cooling these powerhouses has never been more crucial. And so, we delve into one of the hottest (or rather, coolest!) topics of today: Liquid Cooling Mastery - High Performance Systems. This Special Report has been tailored specifically to demystify the seemingly intricate concept of liquid cooling. Whether you're a seasoned IT professional, or a curious enthusiast, navigating these systems can seem like delving into deep, uncharted waters. Shining a light on these intricacies, our report focuses on making the technical digestible. Our aim? Guiding you along the journey of understanding the function, design, and effective implementation of these systems. So, buckle up as we embark together on this voyage through the landscape of liquid cooling systems. Harness the power of this knowledge, and stand out as a savant in the sphere of high-performance cooling systems.

Chapter 2. Understanding the Basics of Liquid Cooling

Liquid cooling— the method of using a liquid-based substance to reduce the heat generated by a system or device. It dates back to early mainframes when high-powered machines needed a way to dispense the heat they produced efficiently. Over the decades, this technique has evolved and scaled up to manage the heat intensity of our modern high-performance computing systems.

Let's take a slow dive into the fundamentals of liquid cooling. We'll explore how it works, its components, its types, and its advantages over other cooling techniques.

2.1. How Liquid Cooling Works

A liquid cooling system consists of a closed loop through which liquid coolant circulates. The coolant moves over the components producing heat, absorbing it, and transferring it to a radiator, where it's cooled down by fans before beginning the loop again. This constant circulation ensures the heated parts remain at safe, optimal operating temperatures.

The science behind this method relies on the specific heat capacity— the amount of heat a substance can absorb before it starts to rise in temperature. Liquids generally have a high specific heat capacity, meaning they can absorb an ample amount of heat before their temperature increases, making them ideal for coolant systems.

2.2. Components of a Liquid Cooling System

Liquid cooling systems possess a range of components that work together to ensure maximum heat dispersion for high-performance computing systems:

1. **Pump**: Propels the coolant around the cooling loop and plays a significant role in the system's cooling efficiency.

2. **Coolant**: The liquid used to absorb heat from the hardware components. Distilled water or a water-glycol mix are commonly used as they're easily available and have a high specific heat capacity.

3. **Heat sink**: Attached to the component producing heat, it's often made from a metal with high thermal conductivity (like copper or aluminium) to facilitate the transfer of heat from the component to the coolant.

4. **Radiator**: A key part of the system for cooling the heated coolant. It houses fans which cool the liquid as it passes through, readying it for the loop again.

5. **Tubing**: Connects all components in the system, allowing the coolant to move freely. They must be sturdy, non-porous, and flexible.

6. **Reservoir**: This is where the coolant reserves are stored. It helps maintain the coolant volume in the loop and aids with the coolant priming process.

7. **Fans**: Attached to the radiator, these cool the heated coolant before it enters the loop again.

Each of these plays a vital role in harnessing the energy of high-performance computing systems and turning that potentially hazardous heat into manageable, dissipated energy.

2.3. Types of Liquid Cooling Systems

There are two major types of liquid cooling systems: closed-loop (or All-In-One, AIO) systems and open-loop (or custom) systems.

1. **Closed-Loop Systems**: These systems come pre-filled with coolant and are sealed at the factory. They're designed to function without any need for maintenance. The major components — the pump, coolant, and radiator — are all encapsulated in one unit. This makes them comparatively easier to install and less likely to leak. However, they are less customizable and may not be as efficient as open-loop systems.

2. **Open-Loop Systems**: Also known as custom water cooling systems, these are designed for the more adventurous and technically adept. They're highly customizable, have higher cooling efficiency, but require more maintenance. Careful planning on the placement and alignment of the multiple components must be done to avoid leakage, water damage, and to achieve optimal cooling.

2.4. Advantages of Liquid Cooling

Liquid cooling takes the lead over air cooling in terms of performance, noise reduction, and even visual aesthetics:

1. **Superior Cooling**: Due to their high specific heat capacity, liquids can absorb and transfer more heat than air, resulting in better thermal performance.

2. **Lower Noise Levels**: Liquid cooling systems offer a quieter operation. The fans attached to the radiators run at a lower speed and noise level than ones needed in air cooling systems.

3. **Aesthetics**: For those who care about how their hardware looks, liquid cooling offers an aesthetically pleasing setup with clear tubes, colored coolant, and sleek pumps and radiators.

In conclusion, effectively mastering liquid cooling systems for high-performance computing systems requires a solid understanding of the basic principles, system components, and types. It's a journey that requires time, patience, and careful planning, but equipped with accurate knowledge, you're one step closer towards optimal cooling mastery. This tech isn't just for the gaming community or IT professionals anymore — it's becoming a vital part of the high-performance computer world. And with this understanding of the basics, you've set your foot securely on the path. Next, we'll deal with the practical implementation of these systems, solidifying your grip on the realm of liquid cooling.

Chapter 3. The Physics Behind Liquid Cooling

Liquid cooling, often called water cooling, is an efficient and powerful method for removing excess heat from high-performance computing systems. Understanding the physics behind this process requires delving into phenomenon such as thermal conduction, heat transfer, and fluid dynamics.

3.1. The Principle of Thermal Conduction

Thermal conduction, the process through which heat is transferred from a higher temperature region to a lower one in a solid or stationary fluid, is a paramount concept. It revolves around the principle that molecules at higher temperatures move faster than those at lower temperatures.

When a part of the cooler gets in contact with a hot component (like a CPU), high energy particles of the hot component collide with particles of the cooler. This collision transfers energy (heat) from the high-energy particles to the lower-energy ones, causing them to move faster. Consequently, thermal energy is progressively transferred across the cooler's material, distributing the heat away from the initial hot component.

The thermal conductivity of a material measures how effectively it can conduct heat. Metals such as copper and aluminum are common in cooling systems for their high thermal conductivities.

3.2. Heat Transfer and its Role in Cooling

Heat transfer is the movement of thermal energy from one body or system to another. It is facilitated by three main mechanisms; conduction, convection, and radiation. In liquid cooling however, the primary mechanisms come down to conduction and convection.

Conduction, as already explained, is the transfer of heat through direct contact. Convection, on the other hand, is the transfer of heat in a fluid (like water or air) via the fluid's mass motion. When heated, the fluid expands and becomes less dense, leading it to rise against gravity. Cooler, denser fluid then moves in to replace it, creating a convection current.

In a liquid cooling system, both these principles combine to carry heat away from the computing components. The liquid coolant, typically water or a water-glycol mixture, makes direct contact with the hot components (conducts heat away) and is then circulated throughout the system (convecting heat away), effectively moving the heat to a place where it can be dissipated.

3.3. Implementation of Thermodynamics: The Liquid Cooling Loop

Opting for a liquid cooling loop has one sole aim: to move the heat generated by the high-performance system from its source to somewhere it can be safely dissipated. The basics of this loop are simple yet interesting.

To begin, the coolant is brought into direct contact with the heat source by a cooling block, where heat is conducted into the coolant.

The now heated coolant is then pushed by a pump through a series of pipes or tubes to the radiator, where the heat is dissipated into the ambient environment. A fan is often associated with the radiator to help increase airflow and thus hasten heat dissipation.

This cooled liquid is then returned to the pump to repeat the process, establishing a continuous loop of heat transfer from the computer system to the environment. The higher the flow rate of the liquid, the quicker the heat transfer, but also the more power is needed for the pump.

3.4. Radiator: An Essential Component

Despite the deceptive simplicity of the system, the role of the radiator can not be understated. Its design and operation are clever applications of thermodynamics principles.

Composed of a series of small pipes surrounded by many thin metal fins, the radiator exposes a large surface area of the heated coolant to the air. Heat from the coolant is conducted to these fins, where it then dissipively convects into the environment.

3.5. Coolant: The Liquid Conductor

While water ranks efficaciously as a coolant due to its high heat capacity and thermal conductivity, issues with electrical conductivity and corrosion often leads to the use of special coolants. These coolants, often glycol-water mixtures, improve the overall performance and longevity of the cooling system by mitigating aforementioned issues. The best coolant also depends on the specific system's characteristics and demands.

In conclusion, liquid cooling is a highly efficient method of handling the high heat loads generated by modern computing systems. It is an interesting and effective application of the fundamental principles of thermodynamics and fluid dynamics. Keep these principles in mind as you navigate the world of high-performance computing, confident now in your understanding of the cool world of liquid cooling.

Chapter 4. Material Selection for Liquid Cooling Systems

Selecting the right materials for your liquid cooling system is a significant step towards achieving optimal thermal performance and reliability. It's a delicate dance of balancing thermal conductivity, chemical compatibility, strength, cost, and more. This journey isn't about choosing the 'best' material — instead, it's about finding the right one for your unique application.

When selecting materials for your cooling system, several factors weigh in, which we will explore in detail in this chapter. Notably, they include the fluid used in the cooling system, the thermal conductivity of the material, their corrosion resistance, and cost-effectiveness.

4.1. Factors to Consider

Before we dive deeper, it's essential to outline the key factors that should be in your consideration set when selecting materials. These will form the groundwork for our subsequent discussions.

- *Thermal Conductivity*: Higher thermal conductivity indicates that the material can transfer heat more efficiently from the heat source to the cooling fluid.

- *Chemical Compatibility*: The material chosen needs to be resistant to the cooling fluid. Otherwise, corrosion and erosion will occur, reducing system efficiency and lifetime.

- *Strength*: The material needs to withstand the pressures exerted by the cooling fluid.

- *Cost-effectiveness*: Both the initial and operational costs of materials need to be considered. While some materials may have higher upfront costs, they may deliver long-term benefits that offset these.

4.2. Thermal Conductivity

The first major factor in selecting materials for a liquid cooling system is thermal conductivity. It's the measure of a material's ability to conduct heat. Metals, like copper and aluminum, have high thermal conductivities and are often used in cooling system components. Polymers and ceramics, with their relatively lower thermal conductivities, are restricted to components where heat transfer is not a primary concern.

However, thermal conductivity isn't straightforward. The effective thermal conductivity of a material depends not just on its intrinsic properties but also on the way it is incorporated into the system, the thickness of the component, and the type of fluid used in the cooling system.

Moreover, it's not always about picking the material with the highest thermal conductivity. Some high conductivity materials like copper are more costly than alternatives like aluminum that could potentially meet the system's thermal requirements at a lower upfront cost.

4.3. Chemical Compatibility

Aside from thermal conductivity, chemical compatibility is a vital aspect of material choice. A material that might excel in heat transfer could fall short if it reacts negatively with the coolant.

To find a suitable material, you must understand the characteristics of the fluid being used. The fluid's properties, such as pH, concentration of dissolved salts, and temperature, will determine the material's corrosion propensity. In turn, this could affect not only the efficiency of heat transfer but also the operational shelf life of your cooling system.

For example, despite copper's high thermal conductivity, it's susceptible to corrosion, particularly when in contact with acidic or sulfur-containing materials. Aluminum, while prone to corrosion in alkali solutions, performs well in the presence of traditional coolants like water and ethylene glycol.

Plastics can be a good choice for components like the coolant reservoir, tubes, and fittings. They can be chemically compatible with many different coolants, but always make sure to check manufacturer's recommendations.

4.4. Strength

The material's strength is another factor to consider. The system's material should resist deformation under the pressure exerted by the cooling fluid, variations in temperature, and other physical stresses.

Metallic components, being strong and durable, excel in this area. Aluminum and copper have the added advantage of ductility, allowing them to be shaped into complex geometries without fracturing.

For non-metal components of the system, like tubes and connectors, polymers like PVC, polyurethane, and nylon offer good mechanical strength. But always choose materials according to the pressures and temperatures they will face in your specific application.

4.5. Cost-effectiveness

Finally, cost-effectiveness plays a significant role. Going for the cheapest option might sound like a good idea, but the total cost goes beyond just the upfront price. Consider factors like the material's durability, performance, and maintenance requirements, as these will affect long-term operational costs.

For example, copper is more expensive than aluminum, but its superior thermal conductivity may make it worth the investment for high-power applications. Cheaper alternatives like aluminum might suffice for low-power applications.

On the other hand, plastics, while inexpensive, may not last as long as metals and could require more frequent replacements, increasing their lifetime cost.

4.6. Conclusion

In conclusion, the choice of material for a liquid cooling system depends on a careful balance of various factors. Understanding the trade-offs between thermal conductivity, chemical compatibility, mechanical strength, and cost-effectiveness is key. There isn't a one-size-fits-all answer, but with careful consideration, you can find the right materials suited for your application. In the following chapters, we will explore the specifics of some common materials and their best use cases.

Chapter 5. Designing High-Performance Liquid Cooled Systems

In the quest of managing heat in high-performance computing systems, the key lays not only in understanding the basics of liquid cooling but also in mastering the art of designing effective, high-performance liquid-cooled systems. This endeavor necessitates an understanding of elements that span physics, thermodynamics, and mechanical design. It encompasses integrating these within the broader framework of the system architecture, keeping in tune with the need for optimal performance, efficiency, and scalability.

5.1. Understanding the Basics

Liquid cooling, a method employed to reduce heat in computers, operates on the principle of conduction and convection. Here, heat is transferred from the hot components to a liquid, usually water due to its high thermal conductivity and heat capacity. This liquid is then cooled using radiators before it's circulated back to collect more heat.

The effectiveness of this method is primarily due to the fact that water can transport heat 20 times more efficiently than air. As such, liquid cooling is often the solution of choice for high-performance or densely packed systems like data centers, where traditional air cooling might fall short.

5.2. Components of a Liquid Cooled System

To design a successful high-performance liquid cooling system, familiarize yourself with its key components:

1. Heat Blocks or Cold Plates: These are in direct contact with the heat-generating components. They are made of high thermal conductivity materials like copper or aluminum and their job is to absorb heat rapidly from the source.

2. Pump: It propels the liquid through the system. It plays a crucial role in determining the flow rate.

3. Radiator: This is where heat exchange takes place. Fluid, heated by the components, flows through the radiator, where it gets cooled down.

4. Reservoir: It stores the cooling fluid and helps remove air bubbles from the system.

5. Tubing: Consist of durable and flexible materials, they channel the coolant around the system.

6. Coolant: Generally, it's a water-based solution, mixed with additives to prevent biological growth and corrosion.

5.3. Engineering an Effective Liquid Cooled System

Designing a liquid cooled system requires more than just strapping components together, it requires thoughtful engineering to balance the function and efficiency.

1. Thermal Design: It starts by figuring out your thermal needs. Identify the heat-consuming components in your system, such as CPUs, GPUs, and power supplies; and measure how much heat they emit. This would help you determine the capacity of the cooling system required.

2. Component Selection: It is critical to choose components that can effectively handle the thermal load. Consideration should be

given to the type, size, and design of critical components like cold plates, pumps, and radiators; and their specifications should align with the cooling requirements of your system.

3. Flow Rate and Pressure Considerations: Key factors in the design of a liquid cooling system are optimizing flow rates and pressure drops. The aim is to ensure that the coolant quickly absorbs the heat and dissipates it through the radiator. It is necessary to strike a balance between flow rate and pressure drop, as both influence the performance and efficiency of the system.

4. Layout and Installation: The physical layout of the components should facilitate easy installation and maintenance. Plan routes to avoid sharp bends and kinks. The routing should also reduce pressure drops, maximize heat transfer, and minimize chances of leakage.

5. Coolant Composition: Monitoring coolant composition is important as it influences thermal conductivity, flow rate, and also protects the system from corrosion and biological growth.

6. Maintenance and Monitoring: Regular checkups and maintenance help keep the system running efficiently. Pay attention to common signs of wear or failure like leakages, blockages, and diminished cooling performance.

5.4. Adapting to Technological Developments

Finally, keep up with advancements in technology. For instance, Nanofluids as coolant is emerging as a promising field. Nanofluids consist of nanoscale particles (1-100 nanometers) in a base fluid, like water, enhancing its thermal properties. Computational tools for predicting and controlling the performance of liquid cooling systems are also on the rise.

Designing an effective high-performance liquid-cooled system is not merely an exercise in thermodynamics or fluid dynamics, but it encompasses careful component selection, system layout, and rigorous testing. It is a delicate balance of art and science where the primary goal is to maximize heat transfer effectively with the smallest form factor possible while being cost-effective and reliable.

Though it may seem daunting, the upshot obtained in terms of performance gains, scalability, and extended lifecycle of your computing system makes liquid cooling a worthy investment. By adopting a well-thought-out design process and staying aligned with the latest technological advancements, a well-implemented liquid cooling system can significantly boost the performance and efficiency of your high-end computing system.

Chapter 6. Installation Challenges: Potential Risks and Solutions

Installation of liquid cooling systems, despite their numerous benefits, comes along with a unique set of challenges unlike those faced with more traditional cooling solutions. These challenges range from space constraints to the potential for leaks and handling heat loads, among others.

6.1. Space Constraints

Space in the housing unit, which might already be considerably occupied by existing hardware, is one of the most common difficulties encountered while installing a liquid cooling system. The bulky and dense nature of the radiators, reservoirs, pumps, and tubing of a typical liquid cooling setup necessitates larger spatial allowances as compared to air cooling components.

To circumvent space constraints, you could preferably go for closed-loop, or all-in-one (AIO) coolers, which generally come with a smaller footprint. Alternatively, you could implement case modification practices to accommodate your liquid cooling setup.

6.2. Potential for Leaks

The possibility of leakage is a significant concern when adopting liquid cooling systems as water or other liquid coolants and electronic components are not the best of friends. Small installation errors can lead to coolant leakage, jeopardizing the components' integrity and potentially causing a system failure.

To avoid leaks, ensure you maintain the pump's optimal pressure, replace and test all seals and push fittings, and implement leak detection practices such as pressure testing the loop before introducing it into the live system.

6.3. Handling High Heat Loads

High-performance computing systems generate heat loads that push the boundaries of conventional cooling solutions. Liquid cooling's main strength is its ability to handle much higher heat loads. Unfortunately, the high heat loads demand a fine balancing act between flow rates, pressure, coolant type, and the material of the heat transfer components.

The key to handling high heat loads is careful design. System designers will need to not only match the heat removal capacity to the heat loads but also carefully consider and optimize the flow rates and pressures in the loop. For example, increasing the coolant's flow rate can maximize heat extraction from critical components, but it also puts additional strain on the pump.

6.4. Cost

Liquid cooling setups, especially custom ones, can be more expensive in comparison to air cooling counterparts due to the cost of the components, as well as the potential for increased power consumption with constant use.

Moreover, their maintenance can be more intensive, requiring periodic replacements for some components and potential leak checks.

Determining whether the enhanced performance and longevity brought by liquid cooling is worth the increased cost will likely depend on the specific uses and needs of your computing system.

6.5. Maintenance

Maintenance could turn out to be a more challenging task with liquid cooling integration compared to regular air cooling scenarios. Though less frequent, maintenance tasks for liquid cooling setups typically tend to be more involved due to system complexity and the presence of liquid.

To solve the challenge of maintenance, it is advised to schedule regular cleanups and liquid changes. Furthermore, it's crucial to consider silicate and plasticizer build-up which might necessitate specific coolant changes.

6.6. Noise Control

While generally quieter than air-cooled setups, the level of noise produced by liquid cooling systems relies heavily on pump vibration, the speed of the fans, and coolant flow rates. These components could generate disruptive noise if not appropriately checked and silenced.

For noise control, focus on integrating low-noise production components or plan for sound damping measures such as anti-vibration pads and soundproofing the case.

Understanding these challenges will help you make informed decisions when implementing a liquid cooling system. While these obstacles can be significant, they can most certainly be overcome with careful planning, precision, and the appropriate knowledge.

Chapter 7. Anatomy of a Liquid Cooling Loop

Before we plunge into the depths of the liquid cooling circuit, let's establish a foundational understanding. The liquid cooling loop, akin to the circulatory system in the human body, serves the essential function of keeping the computer's heart - the CPU - from overheating. Its components harmoniously work together to circulate, cool and recirculate the cooling fluid optimally and efficiently. Let's delve deeper into each segment individually.

7.1. The Reservoir

The reservoir is like the storage unit for the cooling fluid. In our analogy, it symbolizes the human body's blood reserve. The purpose of the reservoir in a cooling loop is twofold: firstly, to hold the excess cooling fluid, and secondly, to facilitate the removal of air bubbles from the system. It aids in maintaining a flawless, consistent flow of coolant through the loop. A larger reservoir, while occupying more space, provides more fluid capacity, thus helping maintain system stability during peak load conditions, ensuring an uninterrupted and efficient cooling operation.

7.2. The Pump

The primal force behind the fluid movement is the pump. Essentially the 'heart' of the cooling loop, it drives the coolant across the loop tirelessly. Its efficient functioning is critical to the well-being of your computer: a weak or ineffective pump is akin to having a weak heart - both pose high risk for the system at large. While choosing a pump, care should be taken to assess its 'head pressure,' as it quantifies the pump's capacity to overcome the resistance offered by the elements in the loop; and the 'flow rate,' which is indicative of the speed at which the coolant circulates.

7.3. The Radiator

Subordinate to the pump but equally vital is the radiator. This element of the cooling loop is responsible for fanning away the heat dissipated by the coolant - acting as the 'lungs' in our body analogy. Radiators come in a range of sizes, often quantified by their ability to accommodate fans of particular dimensions (like 120mm, 240mm, etc.). Its design is typically an assembly of many hollow pipes flanked by a substantially large area of fins, providing an ample surface area for effective heat dissipation.

7.4. The Fans

Keeping in sync with the radiator are the fans, which blow away the radiator's heat into the ambient space, thus cooling the coolant. Fans, often set up in a push-pull configuration, act like a bellows, driving away the absorbed heat. While higher performance fans can further optimize cooling, they can also bring the downside of increased noise levels. Balancing performance with acceptable noise levels is, hence, important while selecting fans.

7.5. The Water Blocks

The last crucial element in a cooling loop are the water blocks. These are the 'organs,' directly drawing out heat from the components like the CPU, GPU, and RAM, etc. They are intricately designed, with a heat-conductive base in contact with the component and a network of channels allowing the coolant to flow and absorb the heat. A high-quality water block facilitates optimal heat transfer, keeping your PC components safe and functional.

7.6. The Coolant

While technically not a constituent of the 'loop,' the coolant plays a pivotal role in the operations of the liquid cooling system. It is, indeed, the 'blood' that courses through the loop. The coolant's thermal conductivity, its ability to absorb and carry heat, is vital. Additionally, non-conductivity for electricity is crucial to prevent short circuits. Lastly, the absence of corrosive elements safeguards the longevity of other loop components.

7.7. The Fittings & The Tubing

Keeping the coolant coursing through the loop are the fittings and the tubing. They act as 'veins and arteries,' ensuring a seamless path for the coolant. While the tubing offers a channel for the liquid coolant, the fittings ensure a tight seal, preventing any leakage. Note that it is critical that the fittings match with the tubing in terms of diameter to ensure no seepage or spillage.

7.8. The Flow Indicator

While not a compulsory element, the flow indicator can act as a 'doctor,' providing immediate diagnosis and indication of potential failures in the cooling loop. It visually represents how well the coolant is flowing through the system and whether the flow rate is within acceptable parameters. It's a handy tool to prevent potential damage from flow-related issues.

Now, with a better grasp of each component's role and function in the overall anatomy of a liquid cooling loop, you can see how vital every piece is. This understanding can help you assemble, maintain, or troubleshoot your own high-performance cooling loop more effectively.

Remember, maintaining a healthy and efficient liquid cooling loop requires not only an understanding of each component's function, but also a balanced and considered approach to assembly, care, and maintenance. With your newfound knowledge, you are well on your way to achieving liquid cooling mastery.

In the next section, we will delve into the art and science of configuring a custom liquid cooling loop for your high-performance system. Here, nuances of component selection, assembly, and fine-tuning will be particularly highlighted. The journey of liquid cooling mastery continues. Stay tuned!

Chapter 8. Optimization Techniques for Liquid Cooling

First and foremost, it is important to comprehend the foundational elements of optimization techniques for liquid cooling systems. In order to facilitate the immense heat generated by high-performance computing systems, two core strategies come into play: i) Maximized Heat Transfer and ii) Efficient Fluid Flow Management. Each strategy sparks its own set of unique optimization tactics, which we'll delve into in the following sections.

8.1. Maximizing Heat Transfer

One of the fundamental principles of optimizing liquid cooling systems is enhancing heat transfer. This essentially means improving the ability of the system to dispatch as much heat as possible from the hot components to the cooler fluid. There are several ways we can achieve this.

8.1.1. Material Selection

A crucial aspect when it comes to efficient heat transfer is the selection of the right heat sink material. Materials with high thermal conductivity are generally more efficient at heat transfer. Copper, for instance, is often used for this purpose due to its high thermal conductivity, although aluminium can also be used as a less expensive alternative. However, the decision largely depends on the specific constraints and goals of your system.

```
[cols="2,2", options="header"]
|===
```

```
| Material | Thermal Conductivity (W/(m·K))

| Copper   | 401
| Aluminium | 205
|===
```

8.1.2. Optimal Surface Area and Design

To maximize heat transfer, a large surface area is ideal. More surface area equals more contact with the cooling liquid, which, in turn, allows for a better heat exchange. To tackle this, engineers leverage heat sinks with intricate designs, such as fins, that increase the surface area. The design, therefore, plays a critical role in optimizing the heat transfer in a liquid cooling system.

8.1.3. Thermal Interface Material

Thermal Interface Materials (TIMs) are often used to fill the microscopic air gaps between the heat sink and source. They improve the thermal contact and encourage swift and efficient heat transfer. The choice of TIM depends on the heat transfer requirements and should exhibit low thermal resistance.

8.2. Efficient Fluid Flow Management

The other core aspect of optimizing liquid cooling systems pertains to the management of fluid flow, which involves the strategic flow of coolant through the system to carry heat away from the components.

8.2.1. Pump Selection

The choice of pump plays a critical role in efficient fluid flow management. The pump should be powerful enough to drive the coolant in an adequate volume, at an adequate speed, through the cooling system. However, the pump must also balance power consumption, noise, and reliability which presents designers with a complex choice.

8.2.2. Loop Configuration

The configuration of the cooling loop is equally significant. The coolant path should efficiently reach all of the components that demand cooling. Two common configurations are used: series and parallel. In a series configuration, the entire coolant volume passes through each component, ensuring equal heat exchange, but increasing fluid resistance and requiring a more powerful pump. Conversely, in a parallel configuration, the coolant divides between each component, decreasing fluid resistance but resulting in unequal heat exchange.

8.2.3. Temperature and Flow Rate Control

Active management of coolant temperature and flow rate can also contribute to the overall efficiency of liquid cooling systems. This approach includes varying the pump speed or diverting the flow based on system temperatures. Such dynamic strategies deliver cooling exactly where needed, while minimizing system power and noise.

Understanding the functioning of these elements and their strategic implementation forms the heart of mastering liquid cooling technologies. As microprocessors continue to develop, so too must our cooling strategies, requiring ongoing innovation in optimization techniques. It is through the mastery of these techniques that one can truly stand out in the sphere of high-performance cooling systems.

Chapter 9. In-depth Case Studies: Best practices from the industry

Building on your comprehension of liquid cooling systems, we will now delve into five in-depth case studies exploring best practices from the industry. These case studies are designed to provide a comprehensive view of how diverse organizations have adopted and adapted liquid cooling systems within their high-performance computing frameworks.

9.1. Case Study 1: Large-Scale Data Center Adoption of Liquid Cooling

Consider Acme Corp, a tech giant with a massive data center footprint. Faced with escalating server power loads and a commitment to reducing their ecological impact, Acme Corp decided to transition to liquid cooling.

Acme first started with a pilot project, transitioning a single server rack to liquid cooling. They utilized a closed-loop liquid cooling system, ensuring the entire process was self-contained with no chance of leakage. They also identified servers that consumed the most power (and hence created the most heat) and prioritized them for the transition.

Post-implementation, Acme Corp observed, measured, and analyzed key metrics: power consumption, heat production, and overall system performance. While power consumption and heat production significantly dropped, there was a corresponding increase in system performance.

Upon running a cost-benefit analysis factoring in the reduced energy costs, increased system performance, and environmental benefits, Acme Corp expanded the liquid cooling setup to the entire data center. The organization is now experiencing a significant ROI and is well on their path to achieving their sustainability goals.

9.2. Case Study 2: High-End Gaming and Liquid Cooling

Techie Toys, a manufacturer of high-end gaming hardware, frequently faced complaints about overheating, especially during extended periods of gameplay. To address this challenge, they adopted a liquid cooling solution for their latest gaming rig.

Techie Toys chose a sealed AIO (all-in-one) liquid cooling system. The coolant absorbs the heat from the processor and moves it to the radiator, attached at the back of the casing. The fan ensures the heat dissipates faster, keeping the processor cooler by up to 20 degrees celsius compared to an air cooling system.

The roll-out of liquid cooled gaming rigs by Techie Toys was met with great applause by its user base, with anecdotal reports of reduced overheating episodes and higher gameplay performance from customers.

9.3. Case Study 3: Liquid cooling in the Automotive Industry

Speed Motors, an automotive company renowned for its high-performance vehicles, faced challenges keeping their vehicle electronic systems cool. They adopted liquid cooling to handle the heat generated by the onboard processors and sensors for self-driving cars.

Liquid cooling proved effective at maintaining optimal temperatures for the sophisticated electronics in these vehicles. In addition, its silent operation did not interfere with the overall driving experience.

9.4. Case Study 4: Supercomputing and the Demand for High-Efficiency Cooling

National Research Institute (NRI), a non-profit organization, unveiled a new supercomputer, housing thousands of powerful processors, slated to be one of the fastest globally.

Using immersive liquid cooling, NRI implemented a highly energy-efficient system. Dielectric fluid circulates within the secured server enclosures, directly absorbing the heat generated by the processors, then cool fluid is recirculated back.

The NRI's success with liquid cooling demonstrated its efficacy at this scale, setting the precedent for other high-performance computing centers worldwide.

9.5. Case Study 5: Overcoming Heating Challenges in Cryptocurrency Mining

DigiCash, a cryptocurrency mining company, dealt with significant heating challenges due to continuous operation of high-power processors. To counter this, DigiCash employed liquid cooling.

The use of liquid cooling helped reduce the frequency at which mining devices needed to be replaced, directly impacting their bottom line. This made the business more sustainable and cost-efficient, as liquid cooling helped maintain the longevity of the mining machines, enabling DigiCash to increase their profit margins.

These case studies offer compelling arguments in favor of liquid cooling for high-performance systems. Not only does it significantly reduce device heat, but it also increases system performance, extends the longevity of components, and contributes to energy-saving initiatives.

Chapter 10. Maintenance and Troubleshooting Liquid Cooling Systems

Just like every high-performance machine, a liquid cooling system demands regular maintenance and adept troubleshooting to keep it running optimally. Herein, we delve deep into the necessary knowledge and tips to successfully maintain and troubleshoot liquid cooling systems.

10.1. Understanding the Importance of Maintenance

Liquid cooling systems, although highly efficient, are mechanically complex and can be prone to issues if not properly maintained. The regularity of maintenance largely depends on the type of coolant used in the system, the components in use, and the system's overall design.

An improperly maintained system may lead to degraded performance over time, making the cooling system less effective and possibly leading to overheating of the parts it's meant to cool. Worse, it can lead to leaks, which could be catastrophic for the other components of the system or the entire machine. These dire consequences underscore the importance of regular, thorough maintenance.

10.2. Maintenance Tasks and Schedule

There are several tasks involved when it comes to maintaining a liquid cooling system. Here are a few key tasks and the typical timescales around them.

- **Inspecting for Leaks:** Carry out this task every month. This is to ensure that the system is airtight and no coolant is spilling out onto critical components.

- **Inspecting Coolant Quality and Levels:** Every three months, check if any coolant has evaporated or degraded, and top up or replace as necessary.

- **Cleaning the Radiator and Fans:** Every six months, make sure to take out the accumulated dust to ensure their optimal operation.

- **Flushing and Replacing the Coolant:** Depending on the type of the coolant, you could perform this task once a year or every couple of years at most.

10.3. Techniques for Leak Inspection

Leak inspection is a common concern among users of liquid cooling systems. A small leak can lead to disastrous consequences. Hence, an inspection routine is crucial. Here are some techniques to follow:

1. **Visual Inspection:** Regularly look at the connectors, tubes, and radiator for any signs of leakage. Any discolored or damp spots can indicate a leak.

2. **Pressure Testing:** This can be performed during installation or as part of regular maintenance. It involves pressurizing the system and monitoring to ensure there are no pressure drops, which would indicate a leak.

3. **Use of Leak Detection Dyes:** Many coolants have additives that fluoresce under UV light, enabling even small leaks to be quickly spotted.

10.4. Coolant Quality and Levels

The quality of your coolant plays an integral role in the overall performance of your liquid cooling system. It is important to refill or replace coolant as per the manufacturer's timeline, typically every 6-12 months. Here's how to check coolant quality:

Visual Inspection: Observe the coolant fluid for any discoloration, particles, or cloudiness. Such signs may denote degraded coolant quality, warranting replacement. **System Efficiency:** If the system isn't cooling as efficiently as before with no other change, the coolant could be the issue and may need replacement.

10.5. Cleaning the Radiator and Fans

Over time, dust and debris can accumulate on the radiator and fans. Regular cleaning ensures optimal efficiency of these components. Here's a brief guide:

1. Turn off and unplug your system.
2. Use compressed air to blow dust off the radiator, taking care not to damage the fins.
3. Use a gentle brush or cloth to clean the fans.
4. Carefully inspect and reassemble, ensuring all components are securely connected.

10.6. Flushing and Replacing Coolant

Replacing the coolant involves draining the current coolant, cleaning the interior of the system, and then replacing it with new coolant. Ensure to follow instructions provided by the manufacturer for the procedure and the type of coolant suitable for your system.

10.7. Troubleshooting Liquid Cooling Systems

Irrespective of the advancements in technology, issues can arise. Knowing how to identify and tackle these issues is equally as critical as regular maintenance.

Constant High Temperatures: This could be due to insufficient coolant, a malfunctioning pump, blockage in the loop, or a poorly mounted cooler. **Leakage:** If there's dampness around the pipes, fittings, or on components, there may be a leak. Immediately power off the system and investigate. **Pump Failure:** If the temperatures rise quickly after starting the system and the pipes are not vibrating, the pump might have failed. **Air Bubbles:** If there's noise from the system or if it's not cooling effectively, there might be air bubbles in the loop. These need to be removed by tilting and shaking the system gently while it's powered on.

Ultimately, understanding your liquid cooling system's maintenance and troubleshooting can stave off issues and keep it running smoothly. As the power needs of high-performance systems only grow, so too will the importance of mastering the cooling systems that keeps them running optimally.

Chapter 11. Future Trends in Liquid Cooling for High Performance Systems

As the pursuit of ever-increasing system performance continues, the future of liquid cooling finds itself entangled with trends that span industries, from IoT to Artificial Intelligence (AI), cryptocurrencies to quantum computing. Keeping up with these trajectories is essential for any professional or individual with a keen interest in high-performance systems.

11.1. Innovation in Coolant Technology

In the world of liquid cooling, coolants serve as the lifeblood. These are the very mediums that transfer heat from the system's hot parts to the radiator for dissipation. Traditionally, water has been favored due to its high heat capacity and thermal conductivity. However, the future picture may be vastly different.

For instance, nanofluids - engineered colloidal suspensions of nanoparticles in a base fluid - hold immense potential. An augmentation in cooling efficiency can be anticipated by leveraging the novel thermal properties of nanoparticles. Additions of graphene or copper oxide nanoparticles to water or ethylene glycol have shown to outperform traditional fluids impressively. Future research will conjure the optimal proportions and materials to craft the perfect nanofluid coolant.

Additionally, phase-change based liquids, particularly 3M's Fluorinert liquids, offer promising avenues. They carry heat away by evaporating at the hot spot and condensing at a cooler region, leveraging phase change's energy absorption. These fluids are effective, safe, and eco-friendly alternatives, subject to future innovations that can reduce their current high cost.

11.2. Expanding Scope of Immersion Cooling

Direct immersion cooling, although a century-old concept, is becoming increasingly relevant. It involves submerging components in dielectric fluids that absorb the heat and circulate naturally or through forced movement. This approach has potential scalability advantages due to simpler infrastructure, no need for complex tubing, and the ability for denser packing of components, which increases overall computational power within the same footprint.

Particularly in the context of modern data centers, immersion cooling will be pivotal. Like an old concept reimagined, single-phase and two-phase immersion cooling methods are being refined. With increasing densities of electronics and a push for horizontal scaling, immersion cooling is destined to turn heads.

11.3. Reinventing Liquid Cooling with AI

Artificial Intelligence, coupled with predictive analytics, has the potential to revolutionize liquid cooling by ushering in 'Intelligent Cooling Systems'. These would monitor real-time component temperatures using embedded sensors, then analyze and predict thermal loads. Based on this, they could modulate coolant flow-rates and fan speeds, maximizing efficiency while minimizing power consumption and noise. The possibilities are exciting indeed as they potentially lead to self-adjusting, self-improving cooling profiles.

11.4. Quantum Computing and Cryogenic Cooling

Quantum computing represents the frontier of technology, and with it comes the demanding task of cryogenic cooling. Quantum bits or Qubits, even in solid-state implementations, require operating temperatures verging towards absolute zero, in the millikelvin range.

This extreme cooling challenge is met by specialized helium-based liquid cooling systems, capable of maintaining the supercool temperature environment required by quantum computers. However, cryogenic liquid cooling systems are expensive, complex, and have yet to be tested on a larger scale, making it a rich ground for future research and development opportunities.

11.5. Sustainable Cooling Practices

As we progress into the Era of Sustainability, the onus is on technology to deliver eco-friendly solutions. Liquid cooling, by contributing to efficient thermal management, can help limit carbon footprints. The move towards coolants with low Global Warming Potential (GWP), such as 3M Novec, and sustainable power sources for cooling systems like solar or wind energy channels integrate sustainability within liquid cooling.

11.6. Hybrid Cooling Solutions: The Best of Both Worlds

While promising, liquid cooling cannot serve as a silver bullet to high-performance computing's thermal issues. Essential traditional approaches, like air cooling, remain crucial. The future likely lies in hybrid solutions - combinations of air and liquid cooling that exploit both techniques' strengths while mitigating their respective shortcomings.

11.7. Conclusion

In the realm of high-performance systems, liquid cooling continues to underpin the quest for better computing performance. The adoption of advanced coolants, exploitation of immersion cooling, leveraging AI, venturing into the cold front of quantum computing - these elements will shape the future of liquid cooling, dictated by sustainability and necessity. It is an exciting journey, guided by cutting-edge research, innovation, and a thorough understanding of the subject.

Through this chapter, you have journeyed along the future path of liquid cooling. The voyage continues as trends evolve, technologies advance, and new challenges arise. Understanding, anticipating, and aligning with these directions could herald your success in harnessing the true potential of high-performance systems.

www.ingramcontent.com/pod-product-compliance
Lightning Source LLC
LaVergne TN
LVHW051630050326
832903LV00033B/4712